I0200208

"*The present spirit of humanity has commercialism as its crown and materialism as its throne.*"

"*…When materialism reigns, and when commercialism pervades all the world, it is then that man overlooks the fact of how he acquires his wealth, and his only object is to become wealthy. It is then that all manner of unhappiness breeds in the multitude and among individuals.*"

Hazrat Inayat Khan

Also by Cecil Touchon

Sell People Things They Don't Need

Is it Necessary to Say Something?

The Gayani Meditations Vol. One

Bedtime Stories

The Cut and Paste Poets – An Anthology of Collage Poetry

Important Documents of Post-Dogmatism

The All New and Improved Neoist Manifesto – A Trans-Lingual Edition

The Hidden Sphere of Artistic Concerns

Book Three

Happy Shopping!

Massurrealist Spam Poetry

Cecil Touchon

ONTOLOGICAL

MUSEUM PUBLICATIONS

Ontological Museum Publications

Visit us at OntologicalMuseum.org

ISBN: 978-0-6151-8244-5

Copyright Cecil Touchon 2007 all rights reserved

All rights reserved. No part of this document may be reproduced in any form or by any means without written permission of the publisher.

Cover Design – Cecil Touchon

Cover Art - *Shopping Cart* - James Seehafer - digital photo-montage courtesy

ArtsCorp International – artscorp.com

Ontological Museum Publications

Visit us online at OntologicalMuseum.org

Contact: info@ontologicalmuseum.org

Introduction

The following book of Massurrealist poems are made from texts gathered from email spam messages. Spam is unsolicited junk email that is sent out by the billions from internet entrepreneurs all over the world who are trying to sell something, anything via the internet. For the most part their products have to do with sex entertainment and pharmaceuticals, the favorite being pharmaceuticals related to sexual performance such as Viagra.

Spam affects individual internet users like a plague filling their email boxes with amazing amount of junk mail every day. To combat this flood of unwanted mail all sorts of filtering systems have been created to prevent the spam from ever arriving in one's email box. In order to circumvent these spam filters, bulk mail sellers are constantly inventing new ways to fool the spam filters to get their messages through and into everyone's mail boxes.

Various of these techniques include placing random words into an email. Sometimes there are merely 10-12 words in a message with no reference to anything else nor a link to any website. Other times there are random groups of words below some linked image advertising a product. Other times there are various bits of scrambled texts from a variety of sources.

The texts and words from these various types of spam mail are the basis of the poetry included in this book. The poems are not merely the texts pasted onto each page and left in the raw like a found object but always manipulated in some way that seems the most interesting. This might include rearranging the word order, editing the texts down into some sort of a poetic form or compiling things from different messages such as the subject lines of the aliases used by the spammers.

There is not a specific or continual system of construction used beyond the use of spam mail for the source material and each work is approached with the idea of collaging together some sort of interesting or intriguing or for that matter, merely boring work that speaks to the daily experiences of nearly everyone using the internet today.

Hi,

Not very good erecxction? You are welcome

Arson and cursin done with a will
Cause . . .
NOTHINGS TOO BAD FOR THE ENEMEEE . . .

Sheots, I said.

Because I have changed my mind about keeping this thing,

Make sure you buy loose pants to fit your penis.

The mutant cross between sheep and goats

smoke and flame leap out of the rear,

Don't thank me yet.

Because I want your assurance that you will/should be grateful.

Open his mouth wide with pain,

forcing thudded

and [I] had a nice darkness of my own.

Go volunteer.

Iron John interlopers!

I say 'NO' resoundingly to a myth manifest as reality.

So, is everyone out there a nutcase or a weirdo of some kind?

à®¿à ̄§Zà ̄€à®³à ̄,à®²à®•à ̄□

à®‡à®©à ̄□ à®³à ̄□ à®°à ̄□ à®‡à®žà ̄□

à®™à ̄□ à®³à ̄,$à ̄° à®©à ̄□ à®°à ̄□

à®□333332à®²à ̄,eà®° $R

wà®žà®šNà®šà ̄□ à ̄°à®šà ̄,;à®žà®ƒwà®□3

à® ̇à ̄□ à ̄®à®"-yà®Š

à®Š5.Sà®žà ̄□

à®¸à®®à ̄□9à ̄®; à® ̈à ̄,PRà® ·

à®œà ̄□ à®µà ̄□ à ̄Rà®œà ̄□ f5à®šà ̄□D{

à ̄ªà®‡[à®•à ̄□ à® ̇à®¸kE)!

à®¤à ̄□$2â€˜ xP

à®žà ̄□[à®œà®Ÿà®¿ !

à®•à ̄□ à®µà ̄□â€™ `à®•à ̄□!à®°à ̄□

à®Ÿ à®¸

à®²à ̄,à® ̈Kà®®à ̄□à®žà ̄,

à®±à ̄□ +à®•à ̄□à® ̇à ̄□à®µà ̄□à®®à ̄□

à ̄ ̈Hà®Ÿà ̄€à® ̈à ̄□à® ̄{c^à®°à ̄□

à®±â€™à®š à®±à ̄,

à®¸à ̄□à®°à ̄€à®Šâ€˜â€.

â€□ â€□@â€□ Aà®ªT

à® ̇à®°à ̄ª à®±à ̄□,

à®³à ̄,jà®ªà ̄,à®°à ̄□Ml à®žà ̄,à®°

à®‡ à®žà ̄,Ià®žà ̄□ @0ità ̈

à®‡à®®à ̄□[à®¸à® ̇à®ƒ!à® ̄à ̄^u1à®©à ̄□

à® ́à ̄,Qà ̄§à®®à ̄□ ZAà® ·" @ Wà® ́bRà®¸!

à®¸ à®Ÿà ̄€

à®ª à®¿â€™à® ̄à ̄□-à®µà®ªà ̄,

à ̄□à®¿ Eà® ̈à ̄, 06/08/23(Wed) 1:07

Other guile had been tried in vain,

he got a game spoiled by marking them.

We're glad to see that our life has really been improved.

Feel ready for any thing.

Have some fun, and do as I used to with the fellows in town.

Here's ain't nothin' to fear.

He liked your way of speakin'

see by day,

and funny,

that it was a few pages.

[He] had gone to sleep a sadder and wiser baby.

Purified and warmed his heart

till it began to hunger for the food

behind his paper. To this unusual outpouring

we must have a party next week.

Strong repugnance to returning to the room she had left,

he will make a fine man, if not spoiled by petting.

Put an end in the air,

while the other seemed merely to touch the saddle,

she skipped boldly through the half-open folding-doors to behold.

Graduate can be, found especially.

Castle west city centre hill above.

Celebrate stages annual cantor professor worked university.

Early, connected with harvesting.

Sometimes referred Hanoi's ironic play words referring.

Other, last modified in January.

Referring Hanoi's ironic word play?

Speaker graduate.

Center pietism played important.

Term history main?

When annexed together world war?

Population market.

Became bishopric century remained, so until when.

Ruin centuries rebuilt today.

Art salt.

Also called

River population history main.

Cantor worked professor university founded.

Especially seen, one leading Nazis successor.

External links edit early connected with harvesting salt.

Originally, mostly just building a church within a monastery.

Discussion this sign create art other.

Sights external early.

Century remained so until when.

I identify myself.

He enjoyed his most spectacular year.

[He] had looked forward gradually and rationally;

blocked and abandoned plans for

a life as a philosopher.

He would never be satisfied

as simply a man.

Exploring the new possibilities,

by means of the continuous massacres

of words and the sounds they make,

losses were in the millions.

The fall

took him to

the place celebrities go to die repeatedly.

Eyes careful,

Viewing design about,

launch synagogue large.

Own along lake isle, mostly cook.

Against functions capable brains direct?

Freaky Friday taking casualties.

Increase lets reduces loss easy.

Came across name Dude.

Direct access anytime anywhere using.

How are shot own poor head age.

Cute, partner bouncing went on forever

Lot, studio including slew boost,

Ass guess insane.

Limp response, from guys naked, beautiful.

Searching related clean diet lite plus skins.

Per each displays additional.

Wow, Thursday. What would George do?

Playground super puppy jiggles.

Crazy car crash here through these eyes carefully.

Give, naughty version taking freaky casualties, excess.

Foreign money was attracted to the United States,
and the previous August
Future presidents
crippled by screams
facing nothing but bleak development.
Only theory
did very well in a real-time experiment.
Heaven had turned into having
a plane to take back and forth
But there was no expansion.
Abandoned plans became established.
Life as a philosopher [of] financial markets.
Moment absurdity pledge person.

Hi,

It is so common to have problems with erecxxtion,
Try VIrAGRA and forget about it

Report first, bark later.
Your new associate never saw me. Within the wood is a slab of rock
that levers up with an opening beneath it.

He went that way.

Shall I?

Hi,

It is so common to have problems with

the exiles on this prison planet.

Forget about it.

It will make an interesting gathering.
Interesting-yes.

But impossible.

None is permitted inside the Pentagon.

Hi,
Great news for you.

This was an individual,

dressed completely in black,

who sat on a little platform

on pulleys to the rear.

This lifted and dropped a small
hammer that banged the starter on the shoulder.

Hi,

Very good news!
A number of them.
Direct from the manufacturer!

Any of the fundamental bands in sight?
Any of them close to this position?

Hi,

It is so common to have problems,
Forget about it heroes!

My companion smiled warmly in my direction.
Pulling his gun a bit out of the holster at the same time,
then letting it slide back.
You do understand that if you breathe one word about our...

It is common to have some problems.
Try and forget about it.

Your attitude is unacceptable.

Answer my question or be punished.
I took a deep breath-and reined in my temper.
I'd like that, as I was fed up with [it] all.

It is common to have some problems,
Try and forget about it.

Because at that moment running footsteps sounded

and a wild-eyed young man burst into the room.
Alarm! Watch! Patrol coming!

(H)[u] [N]{e}[s]

To I-mpact {T}{V}

C*hina You

T,V [C]{p}<.>

S,ymbol: (C)(V)

We (h)[v]{e} a*lready

(e) CYTV'.s marke-t impa^ct

befor^e cl_imb^ing to

{o}[e](r) $*2.00 {w}{i}(t) {e}(w)(s){.}

Pre`ss R`elease:

Chin#a You^TV's Cn

B`oo [W]{e}{b} [S]{i}[e]

Rank,s [N][.]{1} on M.icr^osoft

(L){i}[v]{e}

S^earch Eng`ine

C^nBoo

T^raffic Increas+^es

ne*ws, thi#nk

abo*ut [t]{h}{e}

impa`ct, and

[j](m)

on (h){i}{s}

fi`rst thi*ng

Tomor_r`ow mo`rn_ing!

$0.^42 is a {g}[i]

(f)[t] at [h](i)[s] p+rice...*..

Do (y)(o)(u){r} hom,ew*ork

(a){n}{d}

wat.ch [t]{h}

tra*de Mond,ay morni.ng.

Spammer Aliases

Zion Celaya
Melba T. Carlisle
Fanny Y. Call
Bullock W. Eve
Westlake Q. Fansler
Hodges X. Freddy
Fout A. Golightly
Wynn C. Housekeeper
Parks O. Humphrey
Gregory A. Ik
Lovely S. Mancha
Waldroup D. Padula
Quinones T. Roddy
Charity H. Small
Weeks K. Stanislas
Wilde V. Tirado
Moorehead H. Valdivia
Amoriello Ezekiel
Conveyors G. Spark
Ferguson Guillermo
Shirley Arnold
Sophy Beauregard
Sophia Echols
Stephan Castillo
Stye J. Shipmates
Supermen R. Counterweights
Quickens R. Characters

More Spammer Aliases

Lockman R. Leveller

Bowersox P. Richerson

Brain U. Hans

Clockworks P. Tlingit

Ridgeway T. Osmond

Wimmer O. Madduxn

Ball L. Sloping

Carpetbags O. McGuire

Medicate H. Grandest

Margins J. Cadiz

Ithaca O. Oxygenated

Stiff B. Bare

Brush J. Clausen

Joines A. Bogner

Plunk K. Scalzo

Wales U. Nock

Kawamurag Q. Slavens

Winder E. Escarcega

Napolean E. Guertin

Morehouse V. Wrenn

Gloss G. Pesina

Derry S. Hogan

Stuckey R. Silvey

Batiste T. Basso

Hi,

Not very good erecxction?
You are welcome!
Smiling benignly into his glaring, frozen face.
Due to stay that way for quite awhile.
I turned and waved at my statue-like audience.
The best part was working with
The Stainless Steel Rats.
Thanks

Song carry real ship.

Own children trouble, deep.

Little, sent weight.

Don't short, small port.

Could hat took night.

Result left wind big science build.

At, lone an, vowel.

Exact danger, drop unit, between.

My create short.

Wrote weight food, wall sentence.

Organ deep allow sea ocean.

Copy world together.

Base do, receive, cool saw.

Went miss from number clean, began.

Hot spoke success finger though, again.

Off complete, join fraction but.

Though, together nothing and either.

Wave plain lead took ship.

Morning began, one invent machine, school, number.

They describe water, home long red now.

Crop edge road record foot girl distant.

Song inch wave she at better, take.

Element do so.

Though book old pound.

Miss mean make hour product has.

Knew read general feel.

Down crowd cloud nose, now flow.

Place, deep nothing one unit.

Their, city paint, excite temperature, tire.

One would street held back very.

Heart believe same race learn last trade.

Temperature off made front strange.

Pair check eat heart time.

Help year cold, fill sentence touch.

Plain old horse draw eye, might either.

Eat differ back done like short.

Age that, write too.

Take at own three done, state.

What does your life need?

For someone to, with you, have a great time.

For love to find you.

To get some.

Companionship.

Then you've found your place.

All of these lonely women want to be banged.

German protozoan plaid.

Scenic replaceable sliver.

Airpark do her try,

Academe avoid, scent

Apologetic beheld

Auspicious chinquapin

Assyria convict

Andorra. conduct bilge.

Adriatic crime a construct cottage

Acrylic anglo

Binaural braggart

Billionth disruptive.

Can dogbane

Chuff demurrer

Contralto compulsory datum

Antonio lamebrain deciles askew

Amicable deter business.

Automobile cowpony

Automatic dignitary

Barefaced die

Britannic Canada

Bio-type condition

Courier channel make

Carmichael bias,

Candle lit,

Christy arboretum.

Diabolic aunt currant

Disruption bookend cartridge

Daub decision.

[He] always made her feel as if he was heaping coals

he probably sells them.

this girl writes, and there's a documentary about animals.
I think it would break my heart.

The elbows in suds,

singing like a blackbird

she scrubbed on how sweet she looks tonight!

Waving her hand,
looking with little favor at the new-comer.

To me it seemed that if

loving words were needed,

she spoke.
Good had been seen, remembered.

So don't borrow trouble or

the memory of fear

[He] stood about with his thumbs in the window and looked out.

A hint of evil, only an hour's debasement for him, a moment's glimpse.

He was looking at her as intently as eyes and glasses could.

They go flapping round with satisfaction.

Very little to see, however, only a pretty, a soft.

And if they get out into the light,

that could do it,

as that of a man between a lighted candle and an open powder barrel.

A soft rustle filled the air

[He] uttered a deep, suggestive yowl,

[Her] hero came.

A smile followed, very bright and sweet.

[Think of] all of aunt plenty's new pocket handkerchiefs.

Whistling like an operatic blackbird

by the art table

she exerted herself.
a voice called
which said as plainly as words, "Dinner."

the poor girl

her own fate depended upon the result.

overrun by a crowd of impudent knitting-needles

a brown carpet of pine needles

feeling quite oppressed with the immensity of the work,

her remorse was quite gone.

At that time the state school,
with the razor blade in his hand,
and continued on survival,
words carried great weight.
Gradually,
it simply did not matter
especially swimming, sailing,
he had practiced it
hiding from the
religious acquaintances later in life,
reality became his fantasy
What a startling thought-
talkative spree on him.
no new.
He won respect.

Not very good erecxction? You are welcome -
I ran.

Back the way we had come and through the still open door.
Hoarse, angry cries were cut off as I slammed it shut, locked it.

The thick panel shook as heavy bodies thudded against the other side.

Explain the enormous

solid

outgoing fellow

with a quit air.

I was always under the impression

To cope,

He liked to fight.

He had nimble moves.

He was never seriously beaten.

He had a hard and dominating

brother born in something

others might think

doesn't ring true.

He had taken on the status of folklore.

I believed as a child that I was God.

At the state school

words carried great weight.

they constantly remind me of my limitations.

One thing, my ego suffered an incredible battering.

.

at first

came

the giants

easily

making

their ivory towers.

A conviction about the shape of

reversal.

One of the generalizations

I established

has diminished.

Experience more closely.

would the central banks would now

This meant that

to assume

I am willing

yen

for

buying

a

plane

back

and

forth

between

New York

And

the fall

of

oil prices.

I used to collect
to the extent
that was necessary
but actually
I don.t have
material
needs

To talk to the last minute.

This was very unusual.

He was always Jewish and George liked that.

He enjoyed the chance,

the suspicions and hostilities.

But his life hardly changed,

Others posed no threat

[he was] aggressive with older people.

When survival became an ennobled value,

in cash distributions as well.

George did not look,

he beamed.

In the years
that followed,
the war was unforgettable.
No sign,
he offered
no dismissive gesture,
no footnote
until the age of [the] Soviet Union.

Survival,
no matter how unpleasant.
Nothing made him feel.
Tricky meant not following convention,
not playing those people.

The rules.
Indeed.

deemphasize clockwork

choreograph curvilinear.

cunning circumstance

chastity corkscrew

cinematic digress

dependent accomplice

disambiguate credo

alliterate anathema

contemptuous cheat

breathtaking bootlegger

abominable counterfeit

delinquent disciplinarian

brimful ammunition

cowpony cart

acculturate document

autumnal aggressor

Be incomplete you
May be incomplete you!
May be incomplete you, can,
Also see grouped, by.
paper compiled,
all books this, to.
And criticism
virtual, texts
and annotated!
added of is.
isbn!

can also see grouped, by subjects.
Stay theory and criticism

prepared for the purpose,

not being used to laborious work,

when she is asleep

and the first thing she looks upon

to strike up and

when they were going away,

turned back to speak

to the amazement of all

turned his heart from his wicked design.

as they thought upon an empty chair,

which proved to be gold.

took it for a fit

of him

she cried out, Both, both!

he did the thing

in the recesses of the cave.

Drew Barrymore.
reserved policy
sexiest, women.
Nelly Furtado,
Sharon Stone
Kate Moss
Jennifer Lopez
Anna Kournikova
Britney Spears.
Angelina Jolie
Shakira Mebarak
Mira Sorvino,
Gwen Stefani
Gwyneth Paltrow
Russia photo.
Air piper
Here for the text only
Halle Berry,
world.
Cameron Diaz

Hi,

Economize up to 50 % on your R X with us
behind the closed doors of our quarters did we let go.

I nodded appreciatively as I listened

while Floyd swore blasphemously and scatologically;

he had a fine turn of phrase and went on for a long [time].

I'm told this will increase my standing

folks muttered, "but that's just bookkeeping."

"Eh, hmm, nah, doesn't sit right."

don't think there are enough atoms in the universe

Fat_her C*onmee at t*h e
alt*arra-ils pl*aced t_h,e
h*o*s t w-i't-h diffi*_culty
in t.h'e mo'uth
of t*h-e awk+ward o.l,d m+a+n
w-h'o h.a+d t'h'e sh_aky h e_a*d-.

M'o's't of t+h,e*m o.w-e_d
thei.r s+uccess to diff er_ent
a n.d inco+mpatib'le qualit. ies.
J-u s_t a-bove it ther'e w*a s
a cl'eft la.rge enou+gh to h*o-l_d a walnu-t.

W'h+e+n y_o*u c,oncentrat,e on s*ounds
y'o.u realiz*e it is difficul'*t
f,o'r t-h,e brai*n to c+ategori.es
a'l'*l t.h-e sound_s, a n d in a sh-ort
wh'ile y*o_u s-t o'p try_ing.

To reco ns.truct o_n*e or m,o'r'e
unf,*rozen area_s, sel_ect t*h'e recon stru*ct
t+o*o-l (')_, a+n,d h'o,l-d d*o-w*n
t_h'e mo.use butto-n
or d,r-a_g o+v'e.r t*h,e a_r,e*a,.

He w+i l*l be d,e.a*d
bef,ore t,h,e morni+ng.
He nev+er wr.ote or r, eceived a let ter,
a.n,d he ne+ver s'poke w_i't,h a_n y
b,u-t t'h-e neigh'bou.rs, a,n,d w+i+t'h
th_ese, f o+r t_h.e m,o s,t pa-rt,
o+n.l y w-h+e_n drun*k on r*u,m .
N-o*t wel'l," s_h'e am_plif ied, "
+b u.t perh-aps as t,hough y,o+u a n*d I
h.a_d e_njoyed a h a.r_d ni*ght's d+rinkin-g
a d_a,y or t,w.o a'g.o .
I w i.l-l r-efer to t.h.e CC as
T+h'e Int*erlocut or a*n-d to myse lf
as Mr. W'h.y Sto*pover ,
if y,o*u slee_p m.o_s t of t_h e w_a.y
betwee.n t*h-e st_ars.

En*ter H,e.r.e
F o.r Y,o+u,r
F r+e.e Uncenso re,d
Passwor'd-s.

Th.ese Ta-iren nobl.es
h_a d hand'led thei.r
peopl.e ba*dly.
A-n d j.u*s-t h*o w
m a*n'y time s h_a*v,e
I wish*ed f_o'r t+h-a_t,.

I quic.kly co'nclu.ded
t h.a't t-h,i+s m-eant
poi'nts f+o,r me.

I had seen paradisians.

So far, bald heads and gray hair, wrinkles.

Just one more sentenced crook.

Who is going to carry his own pack?

Answer my question or be punished

which will kill you horribly in exactly thirty days.

Change can be postponed

if you are not

beginning to lose patience.

Hurl me across the room to crash into the wall, fall.

You can forget the blindfolds.

Sir, I will look at the artifact and explain its operation.

Open nothing.

That sounds like absolute waffle to me.

The truth now.

Verified files, no fakes.
Voting booth? Select your preview partially.

Malicious, virus, threats, search client, both.
Rubbish quite due.
Privately share friends.

Automate [the] frequent enhancing [of]ever wonder why.

Difference that has been.
Bot usually included, destroy.
So it does not have any.
Shrink magic galaxy partners.
Find, delete fakes.
Difference that has been modified.

Lite revolution, is!

For their sole property!

Soul seek knew seemingly jealously guarding?

Again, poor partial past, archived.

Thought exploits attack.
Minutes, optimizes ensure, silently.
Genius resize easy returns all.

Durable protected wit award.

Released discovered unsigned need.
Rolling controlled fast, took coin.
Oh horde here posted direct connect.
Screaming provoking dreams

Closed down luck discovers.
Footprint Latin systems lets access unofficial top!
Earth black.
Mind struggle stories frame and how shape, punch up.
Arab sees growth threat.

Hi,

It is so common to have problems with erxection,
Try VlxAGRA to forget about it

and documents dancing in my head.
There was no mercy in his voice now,

no touch of the tiniest of iceberg smiles on his lips.

my statue-like

toenails

they were naturally rusty.

I let it pass since there were
a lot more things I would like to know first.
All here in Paradise were possessed of a great depression

when you turned and waved

It's snowing,

What is this [that is] vanishing?

This gap in time,

The air's so balmy

The bees are buzzing.

This season not their own,

and appears from here to be overcome.

Like some poor wounded — long left for dead.

[Like] the motionless farm couple trudging,

Left and right, and far ahead.

Swaying in unison beneath the snow,

My soul lies cracked; and when, in its despair,

A salamander scuttles across the quiet [and]

Seems reflected in the infinite.

Where does this all end?

It's [always] returning.

Yes. The obvious

Snaps of ice cracking in the hidden air.

Covering the land

until I am

the sputtering, smoking fire

To reach out into its own vanishing.

-

Hi,
Not very good erecxction?

You are welcome
conference table and sat down in the single, high-backed chair there.
With a wave of his hand he indicated the two smaller chairs before us.
Sit, he commanded.

Behind us was a clank and rattle, a hiss of [steam]

She leaned forward,
resting one elbow on fear
her knee supporting dry the chin
change on the raised hand.
After "To die."

He rattled on,
telling anecdote after anecdote;
now of seldom scissors,
the Argentine war,
now selection of bravely,
the Brazilian expedition.

"I heard that you called to-day," he said,
cutting short the overdone effect
Governor's speeches; polite slight.
Destruction with a idea.

First thing Mon. morning.
imagine everything swallowing;
a form of suffocation.

There escapes a yellow creamy,
or a brown syrupy fluid.
In pure culture
disintegration develops slowly
becoming aggravated by movement,
or by handling,
and are worst at night.
There is redness
the overlying of soft parts,
and swelling with vague fluctuation.

goosefleshy gooseflower
goosefoot goosefooted
are followed by the formation.
such as frequently occur
in the use of exploring needles
attended with any escape
at the point.

This is an odd conversation.

Say most clearly

[What is it] they are talking about.

Way into discourses that

So sorry if I upset anyone

Other wile had been tried in vain,

he got Archie to propose a game

we're glad to see

that our life has really been improved

passed below,

and M:

spoiled by marking them

and Christie felt ready for any thing

have some fun,

and do as I used to with the fellows in town.

Ain't nothin' to fear.

he liked your way of speakin' fust rate,

good-night, my dear, good-night.

See by day

fever had done before it,

and funny,

that it was evident

Polly's sense of humor was strong.

A few pages

had gone to sleep

a sadder and wiser baby.

So held, John had waited with
has been, who "i forgot it."

and Jo took heart again,

for him purified

and warmed his heart

till it began to hunger for

the food behind his paper

to this unusual outpouring with a sense of discomfort.

We must have a game party next week.

She had left,

Rachel with satisfaction.

[though] soft

He will make a fine man,

if not spoiled by petting.

[He has a] strong repugnance to returning

[which] nearly put an end to his velocipeding forever.

Slipper in the air,

while the other seemed merely to touch the saddle.

She skipped boldly

To the room

through the half-open folding-doors, to behold.

However,

was very little to see;

only a pretty Gabrielle dressing.

Hi,
It is so common to have problems with erxection,
Try VlxAGRA to forget about it

she kissed me warmly on my cheek.

My arms embraced her in automatic response,

but closed on empty air since

she had already whirled away and dropped onto the couch.

affinity

Ababa

antonym

agouti

asterisk

bandage

Antwerp

Albanian

acerbic

backhand

airstrip

anthem

bail

arch

arbitrary

fool

antagonist

stigma

Annie
aide
badland
Arab
band
Arizona
analogy
assiduous
Baxter

avuncular
Angelica
aster
anybody
agitate
acuity
armful
aeneid
astray

amp

audition

Auriga

basketball

ameliorate

aleck

abide

Bar

apology

Alden

amiss

artwork

ballot

bah

absolve

Alsop

amanita

alliterate

Hi :)
I'm young girl from Ukraine and need for relations.
My name is Isida and I'm 23 y.o.
See my pics
I'll be waiting! ;)

Wheel mouse compare

move beyond

Highly recommend

Common window so focus content

instant quickly

workaround stay until issues.

use flip navigate through open

cut above usual third

Idiots service who stated

important data whether

while analysis during supposed.

since days ago chance, here!

job producing highly.

Fixed tool competing

Weight currently can be.

existing good luck

Analysis during supposed alert

Bloom Boucher,

Bridgewater anti-Semitism academe,

delft direct.

Birthright crumble crumple at

arid capitol arsenal.

Against bespectacled crass cannonball.

Contemporary Abernathy,

dichloride Bausch.

Beatific chauffeur concerti.

Ambiance archery acts.

Culbertson clod canister credit

Ate armature.

codetermine cleanup.

Cavalry cinnamon chalice

anchorites

contrition contour.

connect auction

ad joint

hydrochemistry

derrick corrugate

belt

Andes discovery.

arc length

Cervantes correlate

afresh bud

disciplinary

diagrammatic.

Diane but,

base ceremonial actress,

Braille alumnus.

Deputy Barton calligraphy bring

cater automatic crypto-analyze.

Disney bridge water chapter

one burnt ban

apple by

breakup blimp clipboard.

Detach breakup cod beyond backstage crag.

bullfinch bereave

amoebae conjugal.

brackish agony Amadeus

billet

blowfish crystallographer.

buckeye Aquinas

context

Cambridge

connect chi

dioxide

confuse azimuth.

chance

crawlspace circumscription

Bernadine acquisition

cannery.

arbutus

anti critter

acts barfly cup calfskin

abbey discipline.

animosity beta

baseline

bio-harmonic deed.

Cobb abutted

comfort bacon.

causal acumen

carson copy.

dictatorial

differential

Ammeter condiment,

Circle bootstrapping cia,

Bat man beginner.

Bug-eyed alizarin amino cloak.

Corsage dick chisel cavern.

Adrift carrageen,

Confine blasphemous crowberry clitoris church goer.

Ah asylum

Basswood antagonistic crayon.

Debris congested cat.

Contentious delusion being burgled.

average armor

denote disyllable.

architect dandelion asymmetry Bavaria

Alia clockwise.

appertain beauty

bisque bookmobile

adagio Bloomfield

coworker

Derek aggravate.

corporeal

armload belt

aqueous Atlantic

dingy

borderland.

I thin,k o u,r fello-ws
a+r-e asle ep.
T e-a r t*h'e-m ap_art
l_i'k,e a flo,ck of d o*g*s
k+ills a w*o.l+f+.
T.w_o or thr-ee of u's ,
carefull+*y se-lecte.d,
wou-ld h a v+e take.n M_oe's pl_ace
advis i*ng a*n-d gui-ding h+i,m-.

Y,o.u c.a_n c.onfi.gure
t'h.e lay,out a-n+d s o+m.e
othe'r opt'ions to a_dapt it
to y*o'u-r nee+ds.

Electric trumps five year NBC Fridays troubled.

hostess styles foody.

Developer conflicts more

comment favor likes Michigan Minnesota, crying.

Occur ring back code sampler alerts stay

Tab looking better option install visual edition.

Hand videos, reside thank god itself.

Able objects browser aware.

Built in anyway oh thingy kind,

fun kuhzillion bug?

cocaine year stump lily ratings.

Agreements entered kindle.

Cocky impression

hers hoping seemed earth.

Rocky fab

outfit articulate earned lost.

Strategic budgeting reporting predictive.

Wysiwyg, quote what get.

Edition studio name

thanks reading manager.

Carol gist was is tall lows pm first congrats lovely sc.

Ago truly, generates whole frank.

Predictive analytics quotes course consulting partners.

Stick sole.

news forge, fresh meat surveys jobs new.

Talked.

Runner coached, daughter, Joyce.

Cure disease opinion nor creates dear ready,

exactly successful profitable.

Utilities internet reviews.

Than cheap easy women!

June April March

so anyhow promoting?

Walking by second picture think.

Sparked rumors after being pictured wearing, baggy tops!

February turns on more than, cheap easy women.

Happen naturally said interview TV.

Wanting to adopt child someday doesn't, happen, naturally.

Baggy tops, in recent weeks apparently!

Knock nooooooo problem

however better before too late.

Who nine years junior made, no.

Breasts look great stops bikini.

Seeing, boxers bunch, thought had bad.

Even there, need I'd

knock nooooooo problem.

Taste their, side ultimate turn seeing.

Someday doesn't happen naturally

said interview TV extra definitely.

Junior made no secret desire.

Anyhow promoting, movie xmen doing job!

Pictures are new or!

Sparked, rumors after being pictured wearing baggy!

Someday doesn't happen naturally.

That's what cant wait see this kid ends up.

Want conflict interests, BTW more gov.

Little dude walking by second, picture.

Expression little dude walking.

Reports year old actress has sparked rumors after!

Give taste their side ultimate turn?

Especially last week she was.

Bunch, thought had bad didnt go though.

What can't wait see this, kid ends.

Know these pictures are new.

Be pregnant with, superior baby Tuesday.

Nooooooo problem

However better [than] before.

Fledgling, bump from prying eyes.

Tease challenge join Hollywood's latest trend.

Thought, had bad didn't go though - sad.

Workers employers abiding basic,

standards specifies certain sectors?

Host friendly infected?

intended preventing attacks!

Start setup clicking downloaded edition.

Buffoonery formerly growth.

Note refresh, original would expire fools joke, wed.

Bringing bear peg the prolonging imbalance market.

Day may board big Joe accurate.

On whew of your!

worked thanks HDTV.

Lab needless how looked might.

Defer, expertise concluded who rolling news a divided.

Officially, presents update non package, calendars web access.

Tool justifies brutal showdown,

averted now may CNN the, stared.

Above fray marvel foresight!

Reexamine methods friend keep signs pact arguably.

Holds my, feeling skin ID, prefer hedge.

Most want installer install whether installed!

Clause strict drugs decidedly, exchange down may, piece just times.

Level, fear deals contract?

Languages remote tools.

behind slide drum latest.

Same sex some how, recruit silly slippery?

Returns coupled increasing securities,

Holds my desire sir waver molesting pack.

Got void warranty beware proceed email apple.

experiment with alternatives.

The fact that one can actually

their threat to your health

Luckily, there is an increased

and with computers is different than it was twenty years ago.

substitutable occupations will be diminishing.

Operators and for land and space.

May be the environment can be saved from Fans

of virtual reality are trying to convince people

that its' prerequisite implemented in our education system.

That is until computer screen accomplishing nothing,

to sitting long hours of schools

will be partly financed by local industries that rely on substitute

for the drugs I've never done

though overloads do yet to reach its full potential.

I can only imagine what future produce

a cleaner more precise product in a fraction of the time.

effects is astounding.

New methods and techniques arise daily

as have most definitely made an impact in this industry,

whether its watching my grandfather reconstruct archaeological sites

and global village, how is the arts the groundwork of culture and

real interaction that fuels my art.

I have found it intriguing to access speech synthesizers,

he learns to speak.

into associating it with virtual reality.

It is ridiculous that newer model computer.

I then decided to investigate a little more

Email system in their organization.

Individual booths will have my language.

We are always partaking in our society

to one's walls at home - it can be displayed in a gallery

or reproduced the whole picture of a controversial issue

which provides the implication that companies will have greater flexibility

in regards meaning

put in situations where they had to pretend that virtual mirror.

When one chooses to buy an item he/she will

A trend that seems to be occurring rapidly

gives rise to a company logo

had to be projected on a wall with an overhead

obviously be the biggest influence in the educational system.

Anyone has the capability to access almost anything from touch.

They will cater to the customer who still enjoys the look

artist has used to create his/her work,

just like a camera, or a condition I call hyper-awareness.

Anything and everything my five artists, even today,

who deal with this same debate.

I usually do not enjoy because it confuses me.

Group policy

while that would seem to makes sense now

The system within the system comes up a lot faster.

I'm not a player.

Victims who get blown away are simply represented

by indistinct red splotches.

i just wanted to say how pleased I am with the training kit.

And yet, the huge success is only going to help reinforce that stereotype.

Even though certification has been a powerful advancement

It has not been smooth sailing in all cases.

If you are investing the time and effort to

The real thing, build your own!

There's normal.

Forbidding one thing is good enough for politicians.

Oprah's boot camp diet.

divisive arsenal

cryptology befallen devotee

degenerate centrist burlesque

delirium

cheerlead demure checkerboard.

better button atheist

diamagnetic belladonna

affiance.

continuo bender

connubial clench blot

component bookie.

abode chub

debugger confectionery

caliper

contentious ale.

bloodbath

conclave confess

cottony

cookery

countrymen.

Hi,

Economize up to 50 % on your R X with us
about the . . . execution.
Do you want to know?
Not really.

Discover how one man is using secrets

to dramatically increase his choices with women.

What's the best way to prevent this?

And make jokes about it.

The answer is simple: they do not have the right information

Secrets of personal authority.

And this wasn't an isolated event.

" The truth is, it is embarrassingly easy,

IF you know what you're doing.

Few, very few, choose the option to destroy the criminal

because they just don't know how.

I've been broke and I've had money,

I'm here to tell you, it's better to have money.

Money makes things better all the way around.

Teaching a truth in understanding how to create attraction

and I'm getting results like never before.

But for now, have a look at, what these guys have to offer.

Get Beautiful, Desirable Women to Chase You.

Wouldn't it be great if there was a sexy women pill?

"Would You Like Desirable Women RIGHT NOW,

Eager to Meet in Person?

I hide the fact that I do OK for myself, money-wise.

An amendment, freedom providing.

Suspects such anyone could.

Data must be made.

Expected Wednesday from clutch worm!

Old when other avenues had.

Launching attacks recent also stopped trying.

Resources power center sponsors preparing enterprise.

Fire, start.

Vista what expect, myths available?

Yours has become my valuable tool.

Evolution finding value so a spectrum common questions benefits.

Exchange automated reporting.

Lot easier to identify photo.

Sharing illegal stuff similar content dismissed moral high.

Creating hard tell same wrote guys.

Power center preparing network curve.

They will, get short, break Tuesday.

Messages, hidden inside claim, do any!

Solution ensures securing automating optimizing learn!

empower fest
magnetite invariant
magnetite track
empower bundle girlie
falconry patentee evasive
planet break excursion
break above cheetah

above sucrose
track subsume memoir
girlie contraband

exculpatory evasive
exculpatory excursion
candlestick contraband

Gets a value indicating whether the [cart] is empty.

Or that I don't cost anything.

You're practically there anyway.

I can't let you go getting chokey.

And no doubt by this time the Feds know it, too.

The main street crooks

pretty sharp right in the business end,

and crooks neither [know] time or two

trying to get out of the first crook.

In the event of an error, return a pointer.

Test this by executing.

This control allows [one] to insert combo-boxes, etc.

drosophila storeroom inveigle paranoia serviette weave
lend whipsaw weave

orthodox cafe wig

drier inveigle seaside inveigle jackdaw pivot drier
osmium heterogeneous paranoia
advocate osmium wig slang flinch serviette weave
lend paranoia inveigle whipsaw orthodox
advocate osmium advocate jackdaw

sourdough detergent upstairs abscess dissemble

sourdough abscess choreograph savant riotous conclave

savant detergent prayer cofactor rheostat prayer

navy clarinet

breeze cofactor homecoming

flattery prayer riotous secrete riotous

upstairs aboard abroad

mush lose

decontrolled decode

tread

offset southpaw

mine

scent in airstrip air strip cost cryogenic prophylactic cost sham

tip off caribou scrutiny develop tip off

sunshade secretariat intoxicate

sunshade shank infighting tetrahedral

tread tetrahedral

develop bi-connected sham

intoxicating earthworm scent

adulterous cream ordinance decontrolled bi-connected

ordinance ethanol tip off cost tetrahedron cream prophylactic

sunshade incapable secretariat tread airstrip

sham shank infighting

earthworm incapable mammal scent

caribou cream incapable bright mammal

cost scent offset

decode tread

azure tampon misanthrope euthanasia

tampon starlight aqua spawn seven

godlike referential resolution

azure presumed starlight

caveat contrary

leftward starlight stricter widowhood

facile starlight chaise stricter resolution

revolution caveat pictorial alumnus

depute aqua gunny audience stricter

alternate hydrate seminar infighting vale autoclave buddy buddy
autoclave muck papal muck dentistry chock muck

alternate seminar
pizzicato buddy multiply Willie Willie
chock stolen

membrane dentistry stolen operable alternate autoclave stolen
rider seminar pizzicato infighter multiple operable breast

butch vale crucifixion taboo tableaux crucifixion

membrane seminar papal stolen

convenient muck t elastic ogress o yacht butch buddy regulate

muck yacht

sidle seminar papal butch fin sidle aspirin aspirin pizzicato

yacht chock incur membrane autoclave

incur cadaver sidle heartbreak benevolent virtue

pizzicato elastic a

dentistry chock papal t stolen papal flirt pizzicato stolen

elastic cadaver muck

taboo cadaver hydrate rate punditry aspirin multiple multiplex

alternate aspirin chock sidle papal ogress dentistry chock

stolen rider breast born operable

taboo dentistry seminar virtue they'd punditry vale

flirt autoclave sidle incur ogress chock in fight

elastic benevolent buddy

bind boulder extravagant floodlit harmonious
pollutant decision making pessimism tying
absentminded decision maker disperse boulder
taxation floodlit neoprene lagoon
tying top concertmaster pollutant
glucose absentminded guideline

declaratory concertmaster brain parabola goggles

gag writer jack teeth mar harmonious disperse

floodlit top
suspect guideline pessimism loquat renal

writer gag renal stint neoprene

recompense bind grub decision make

grub top grub elution pessimism symbolic

guideline grub quetzal declaratory stint

taxation declaratory reticent pollutant

glucose braggart teethe brigade floodlit divine

suite

brigade bind

consul elution elution elution

incline fusion inland tribal dervish urine system
latch pealed perk

wee scrawny rose pealing peal shown
frizzle yourself stew peal limpet tribal falter

brunt fusion trivalent inland system
kangaroo audio
urine yourself crappie limpet
dexterity

latch temple limpet mishap

frizzle incline falter

bug peal curtsey evince tribal pealing

faltered superannuate

audio trivalent crummy biennium stew

rose bootleg crummy shown icon triangulate happy

crummy triangulate dervish fatty evince dexterity

biennium dexterity incline

weak crummy rose morocco frizzle falter

acquaintance peal rose

wee latch temple limpet hap frizzle incline

falter

bug curtsey evince tribal

falter superannuate

audio a trivalent crummy stew

rose bootleg crummy la shown triangulate hap

crummy triangulate dervish shitty evince dexterity biennium dexterity incline

wee crummy morocco frizzle falter acquaintance rose peal

spread dart longhand rodent malformation

document conjugal rangeland malformation trait

gabble sovereign font fructose oppressive malformation

last mantissa conjugal aura dart

dart oppressive document malformation rodent

strophe mantissa

win conjugal rodent rangeland

skyjack ferrite aura rodent malformation

intercom fry incompressible stimulate

likewise regurgitate marathon antebellum

grainy we foreign beryl raise

beryl pilgrimage conspicuous perspicacious earl

conspicuous hawthorn navigable defect navigable

defect earl padre foreign

marathon incompressible intercom we

intercom stimulate perspicacious congregate perspicacious

conspicuous congratulatory regurgitate

workstation stimulate perspicacious grainy likewise earl

earl fry flask grainy congregate

solicitude beset belief accessible patch consume edematous derby fearful

economist andesine derby teat adverb cinquefoil beset hoi

beset andesine fabulous cinquefoil judicable

cartilaginous

cinquefoil cartel nun fearful phone judicable

confusion fabulous cartilaginous capstone beset

cartel derby cinquefoil

derby hierarchic adverb teat beset cinquefoil capstone judicable

patch twentieth economist

almond gentility scar
inaudible defrost
dressy wet celebrity inaudible
celebrity dobbin silhouette firemen fickle

visor firemen gentility wet
citation yarn exclaim
visor leukemia separate bindle
resplendent firemen bondsmen

other world pick axe resplendent

exclaim dodecahedra vulture visor vigilant fickle groove s

groove fickle bondsmen defrost vigilant defrost ribosome basin yarn

ribosome celebrity

plantation silhouette leukemia almond inverse defrost

shoal rebellion separate dobbin batwing welfare shoal bindle tome

gentility inverse silhouette batwing

celebrity dressy plantation dressy bindle

gently roll down my cheeks,

i love playing,

patronage mustard risky audiotape refrain

trio tight vista octahedron mix up

vista edgewise porcupine grateful

patronage tone butterfly exultation savagery

tight exultation impiety my

my risky audiotape grateful

porcupine gnome lest

mustard refrain risky patronage

grateful underling exultation tone innermost

sum impiety water audiotape

piety embedding risky compelled patronage

patronage octahedron savagery mix-up exultation

octillion footman spherical footman

vertigo wardrobe black jibe

pioneer titanic genital

tenth socket languish

quintessence melt water

spherical carpenter soiree

shrubbery footman tenth drainage jibe

slop hoot foundling rust genital foundling

wardrobe vertigo spherical socket

socket

www.ingramcontent.com/pod-product-compliance
Lightning Source LLC
Chambersburg PA
CBHW030419100426

42812CB00028B/3023/J